Nexus Investing

(How to Beat the Market)

By

C Lighthall

Dedication

Dedicated to Alan, the real investor in the family

Table of Content

Preface

I was 30 years old when the thought occurred to me that there were few things in life that would be worse than growing old and poor. I calculated how much money I would need to save in order to be comfortably retired by the age of 55. I set a modest standard of living, a modest investment return on savings, and calculated how much money I would have to accumulate in order for it to last from age 55 to the end of my life expectancy (85). To reach this total amount of money I calculated an annual savings rate based on a percentage of my annual income and modest investment gains on my savings over the decades. Fortunately, this is not rocket science. There are standard math formulas for these calculations.

Fast forward 25 years and my dream came true. It happened quite a bit differently than I had anticipated, but then life rarely goes the way we planned! The company I worked for handed me a mandatory early retirement due to a series of corporate mergers, consolidations, and layoffs. Fortunately, my planning paid off and I was able to afford to retire.

Part 1 of this book is devoted to explaining the basics of financial management and setting up a saving and investing plan for retirement. Part 2 of this book explains how Nexus Investing can enable you to achieve better results from stock market investing than either standard buy-and-hold investing or investing with fixed periodic rebalancing.

Disclaimer

Past performance is no guarantee of future results. The information in this book cannot guarantee that you will achieve the same results that I have, or any specific returns on investment.

Part 1

Conventional Investing

Three Pitfalls to Avoid When Investing

1. Never borrow money to invest
2. Never invest in anything that you don't understand
3. Never put all of your eggs in one basket (diversify)

Never Borrow Money to Invest

Borrowing money to invest is generally referred to as leverage. It is a dangerous practice that you would do well to avoid. You can end up losing the money you borrowed and find yourself deep in debt.

Never Invest in Anything That You Do Not Understand

There are many exotic investment products such as options, puts, gets, hedging, hedge funds and many more. You would do well to avoid these also. Mutual funds are the most simple and understandable investment for most people.

Never Put All of Your Eggs in One Basket (diversify)

We all dream of picking the next high-flying company, investing in it and becoming instant millionaires. The odds are very long (poor) that anyone can predict the next big winner. It is best not to try. It is a quick and easy way to lose all of your money if the company fails. The easiest way to diversify an investment portfolio is with mutual funds.

Three Golden Rules of Investing

Whereas the three pitfalls above told us what not to do, we will now look at what we should do. Three important components to successful investing include:

1. Asset Allocation
2. Diversification
3. Low Cost

Asset Allocation

Asset allocation is how an investment portfolio splits between stocks and bonds. What percentage placed in a stock mutual fund and what percentage in a bond mutual fund. Stocks tend to be more volatile than bonds, yet over the long term tend to produce greater returns. Thus the greater your tolerance for risk and the longer your time horizon (the younger you are), the more of your portfolio you can invest in a stock mutual fund. Someone who has 25 years until retirement could put up to 80% of the portfolio in a stock fund. Someone close to retirement might want a more conservative 50% in a stock fund. The remainder would be invested in a bond fund.

Diversification

Mutual funds automatically provide diversification. A mutual fund is a basket of stocks. A Total Market fund will invest in several thousand stocks. That is basically the entire U.S. stock market. A 500 Index fund invests in the 500 largest companies in the U.S. That encompasses most of the big brand name companies that we all know and recognize.

Low Cost

Index funds provide one of the lowest cost options for stock mutual funds. Since there are no people researching and deciding which stocks to buy for the fund, costs are kept to a minimum. A Total Market index fund is one good choice. A 500 Index fund that invests in the 500 largest companies in the U.S. is another good choice. There are several good choices in bond funds including a short-term investment-grade bond fund or a total market investment-grade bond fund.

Investing Techniques

There are many different techniques for investing. Many investment advisors advocate a "buy-and-hold" strategy. This tried and true method should produce investment returns that match the overall market or match the returns of your mutual fund. This is also called passive investing and does not require any effort on your part.

Another investment technique uses "rebalancing". With this technique, you rebalance your portfolio between your stock and bond funds to achieve your standard asset allocation. You do this by shifting money between your stock and bond funds as needed to achieve your standard asset allocation percentages. Do this as little as once a year or as often as once per quarter (four times per year). This technique should result in returns that exceed that of "buy-and-hold" investing since it automatically buys stocks when they are lower in price and sells them when they are higher in price. This requires occasional active management on your part.

Nexus investing seeks to exceed the returns of both of the above techniques. See part 2 for the details on Nexus investing.

Saving and Investing Steps

1. Eliminate all short-term, high-interest debts (a home mortgage is okay).

2. Set aside 3-6 months' living expenses for emergencies in a money market account.

3. Save money in an interest or dividend paying account (money market or short-term bond fund) for planned near-term purchases of major items such as a down payment on a house, auto purchase, furniture, appliances, etc.

4. Invest for the long term (retirement) through an automatic investment plan.

How Much to Save for Retirement

How much will I need to save for retirement? That is a loaded question. It is a little like asking "how large is an apple?" A lot depends on your lifestyle and your expected lifestyle in retirement. It also depends on whether you pay off your home mortgage before you retire, whether you are finished paying for your children's living and college expenses, etc. For planning purposes, it is safest to plan to pay off all debts before you quit your job and retire. For planning purposes, figure on maintaining a similar lifestyle to what you had before retirement. That would mean the same expenses minus mortgage, children's expenses, and savings expenses. If you want extravagant items, you will have to save extra.

With the above parameters in place, the following general guidelines should get you close to your target. Save an amount equal to 15 percent of your income, every year, for 25 years. That could be 10% of your income in a 401(k) program, augmented by a 5% match from your employer. You should start with an asset allocation of 80% in a stock fund (such as a Total Market index or 500 Index) and 20% in a bond fund. By the time you retire, your asset allocation should be 50% stock fund and 50% bond fund.

The key factor is the number of years you have available to you to save for retirement. The more years available, the more you can contribute and the more investment gains you can achieve. The sooner you start, the easier it is. We could show the math formulas and the tedious calculations that produce these results, but it would probably give you a headache.

1. 25 years until retirement, save 15% per year
2. 20 years until retirement, save 17% per year
3. 15 years until retirement, save 28% per year
4. 10 years until retirement, save 55% per year

As the table above shows, saving for retirement is manageable if you allow 20 years or more. However, with only 15 years or less it is a daunting task! This is largely because of the compound investment gains earned over time. Many refer to this as the time value of money. An investment pundit termed this effect, "the eighth wonder of the world."

Investing Priority by Account Type

1. Contribute enough to your 401K or 403B to get the maximum employer match

2. Contribute the maximum allowed to a Roth IRA

3. Contribute the maximum federal limit on your 401K or 403B contribution

4. Invest in a taxable account through an automatic investment program

Investment Type Matched to Account Type

You will get the most out of your investments if you correctly match the type of investment to the type of account. Try to place investments that generate currently taxable income, such as REIT (real estate) funds, bond funds, and CDs in a Roth IRA, traditional IRA, 401(k) or other tax-advantaged account. Stock funds such as a Total Market mutual fund or a 500-index fund; do not generate much in the way of currently taxable income. Therefore, it is ok to hold them in a non-tax advantaged account (i.e. a regular investment account).

Part 2

Nexus Investing

Nexus Investing Strategy

The key to Nexus Investing is to take advantage of every opportunity to buy stock through stock mutual funds when the price of stock goes down sufficiently. Thus, you are buying stocks when they are on sale. This requires active management of your portfolio. You must watch for and recognize the time to buy. The time to buy is the **Nexus.** The word nexus means "the most important point." The most important point, the nexus, in this strategy is the point at which stock is a sufficiently good buy.

Many people who try to decide when to buy and sell stock do so with too much emotion. When the stock market is going up to new heights, they feel optimistic and buy. When stocks are dropping in price, they become worried and decide that they should "get out" and sell. This emotional behavior has the worst possible effect on returns. They buy high and sell low. This results in disastrous returns. A simple strategy of "buy and hold" or periodic rebalancing would be better than emotional investing.

Investors should recognize that stock is a commodity to buy and sell like any other commodity in our economy. When products that you use regularly go on sale that is the time to buy and stock up (pun intended). When the price of stock drops significantly, rather than run for the exits, perceptive investors should treat it like a blue-light special and fill their shopping carts.

A ten percent drop in the stock market is considered a "correction." A twenty percent drop is considered a bear market. **For the purposes of nexus investing, we consider a ten percent drop in the stock market to be the nexus point to buy stock**. The Standard and Poor's 500 index is a good proxy for the market. It is widely reported on news channels and is therefore an easy index to track. Thus, a ten percent drop in the Standard and Poor's 500 index is the nexus and signals a buying opportunity. But remember, we are not playing Texas Holdem' so be careful not to go "all in" too quickly.

Historically the stock market has experienced several times when it dropped by as much as 40 percent or more. A good rule to follow is to only shift one-fifth (twenty percent) of your bond fund holdings to your stock fund for each ten percent that the stock market drops from its peak. Then you must play a patient waiting game. You must wait for the stock market to recover to its previous high point. That may take weeks (for a ten percent drop), months for a twenty percent drop, or years for a larger drop. If you follow these principles correctly, you can achieve significant gains.

Nexus Investing (How to Beat the Market)

In addition to using the Nexus Investing strategy, do not forget to rebalance your portfolio. If the stock market experiences a significant increase in value, you could have too large a percentage of your portfolio in stocks. If this occurs, move money from your stock fund to your bond fund until you achieve your target asset allocation. This reduces future investment risk and provides you with more cash to take advantage of the next stock market drop with the Nexus Investing strategy.

How often does the nexus appear? There are usually at least two corrections (ten percent drop) in the stock market per year. A bear market (twenty percent drop) usually only happens once every several years. There were two severe bear markets in the first decade of the 2000s when the stock market dropped at least 40 percent and took years to recover. Those bear markets provided the perceptive investor, using the Nexus Investing strategy, with the opportunity to make a lot of money. The Nexus Investing strategy works equally well during the years when you are saving for retirement and after you are retired.

The year 2015 provides a good example of how nexus investing can beat a buy-and-hold or annual rebalance strategy. In the year 2015, the stock market ended, the year essentially unchanged from the beginning of the year. Thus, a stock portfolio using buy-and-hold or annual rebalancing ended the year with no gains. However, between July and October of 2015 there were two separate ten percent corrections and recoveries in the stock market. An investor that used the nexus method to buy on each of those dips and then sold on the resulting recoveries would have earned ten percent on each of the two buy amounts.

Let's look at a specific example for the year 2015. We will use a portfolio with $50,000 in a bond fund and $50,000 in a 500-index fund following the nexus strategy in 2015. On the first nexus signal (a ten percent drop in the 500 index) the investor moved one fifth of the bond fund ($10,000) to the stock fund. When the market recovered to its previous level the investor moved $11,000 from the stock fund to the bond fund. On the second ten percent drop in the stock market, the investor did the same thing again. This portfolio ended the year with $50,000 in the stock fund and $52,000 in the bond fund plus whatever interest or dividend the bond fund earned for the year. The salient point is that the stock portion of the portfolio returned $2,000 to the annual gain of the total portfolio in a year when the stock market had no gain for the year.

Another thing to consider when investing is tax efficiency. Every dollar paid in taxes is a dollar less for you, the investor. This nexus strategy of enhancing a portfolio's returns works especially well in a Roth IRA where all investment gains are TAX FREE. Thus, you get even more "bang for your buck." The next best place to use the nexus strategy is in a tax-deferred account such as a traditional IRA, a 401(k) or 403(b) plan.

Retirement Withdrawal

With life spans in the United States now averaging over 80 years, it may be necessary to fund 25 years or more of retirement. Therefore, one should maintain a long-term perspective regarding retirement investments. This means keeping a portion of your retirement investments in stocks to provide some long-term growth in your portfolio. You should also adopt a conservative withdrawal rate to help minimize the chance that you will outlive your money.

When you first retire, you should have an asset allocation that still has 50% of your portfolio in a stock mutual fund for long-term growth. Most financial pundits predict that with 50% of your portfolio in a stock mutual fund a withdrawal rate of 4% annually translates to barely touching the principle. A 5% annual withdrawal rate translates into your money running out in 25 years.

Even in retirement, it is advisable to maintain a well-balanced, well-diversified portfolio. The Nexus investment strategy will help to guard against running out of money by boosting your returns.

In general, it is best to withdraw money from a taxable account first, while leaving tax-sheltered money to grow tax-deferred. You can make qualified retirement withdrawals from a traditional IRA, SEP-IRA, SIMPLE-IRA, 401(k), 403(b) or 457 plan after age 59.5, regardless of whether you are working or not. You must begin taking required minimum distributions from these tax-favored plans when you reach age 70.5. Withdrawals from these plans are taxed as ordinary income. You can make qualified retirement withdrawals from a Roth IRA after age 59.5 as long as your first Roth IRA contribution was at least 5 years previous. You are never required to withdraw money from your Roth IRA. Qualified withdrawals from a Roth IRA are tax-free.

Rebalance Tax Efficiently

Rebalance your portfolio annually in January or whenever it is at least 5% out of balance. For funds in a taxable account, do not reinvest dividends and capital gain distributions; rather use that money as part of your annual withdrawal amount. You can also rebalance by withdrawing money from investment categories that are overweighed. In tax-deferred plans (such as 401(k) or IRA), you can move money to rebalance without incurring taxable gains.

Nexus Investing (How to Beat the Market)